Bach E Major Prelude from the Partita No. 3 for Solo Violin Transcribed for Mandolin

by Andrew Driscoll

Online Audio   www.melbay.com/30211BCDEB

Audio Content

| 1 | Prelude |

1 2

Visit us on the Web at www.melbay.com — E-mail us at email@melbay.com

Prelude

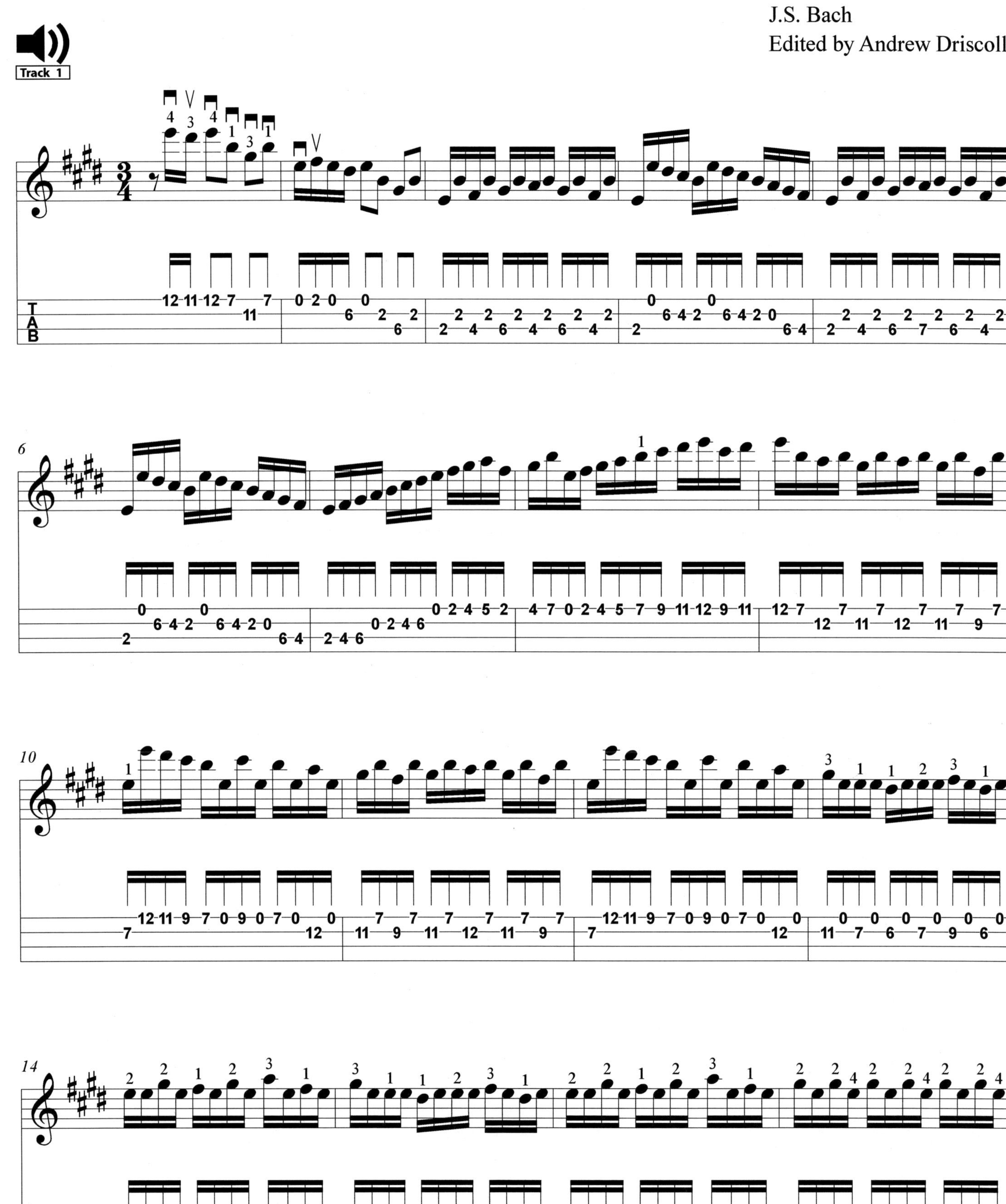

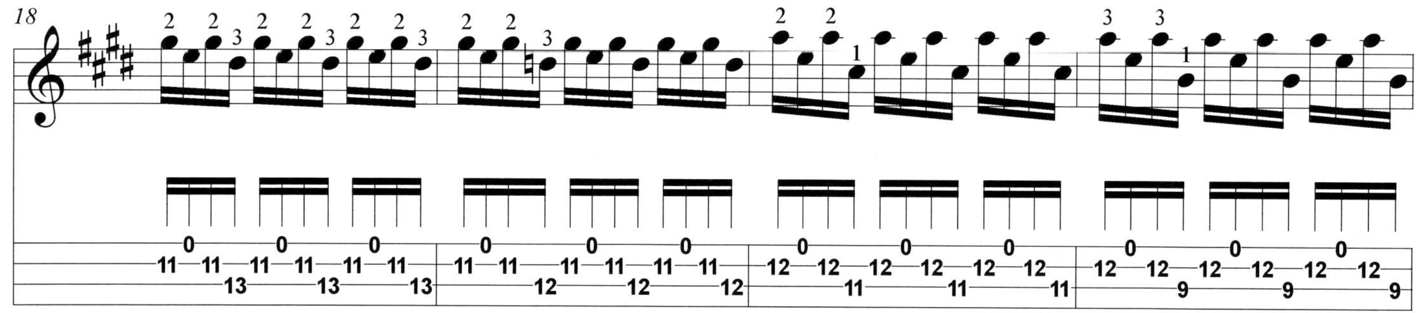
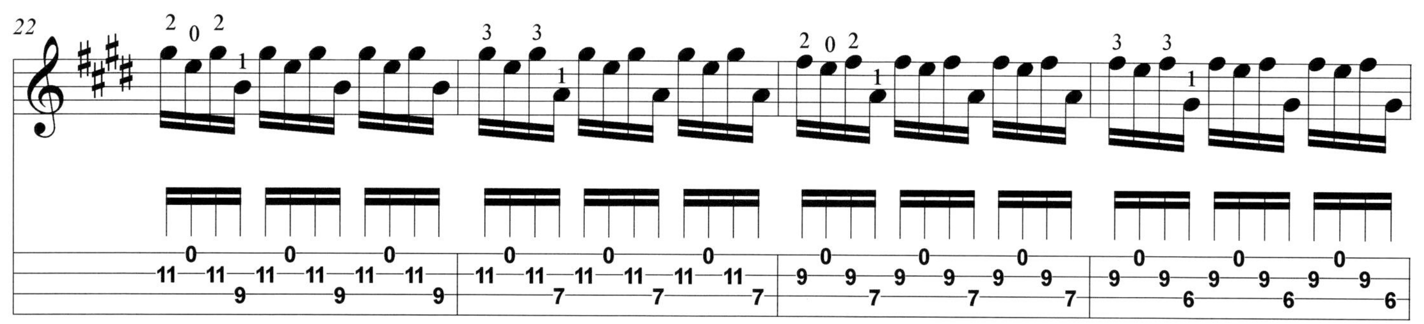
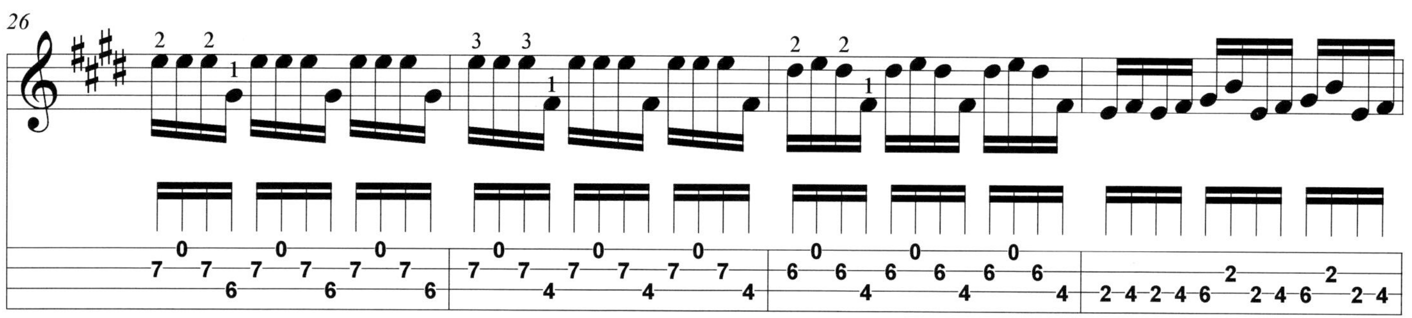
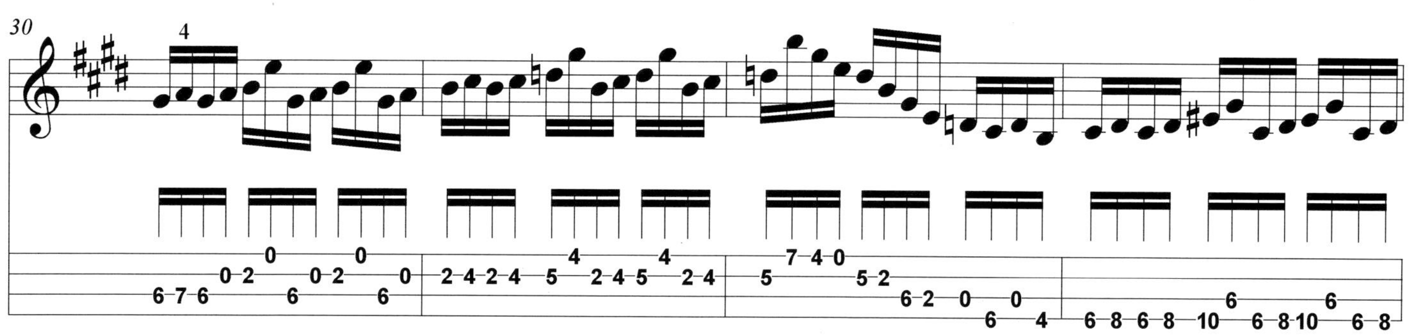
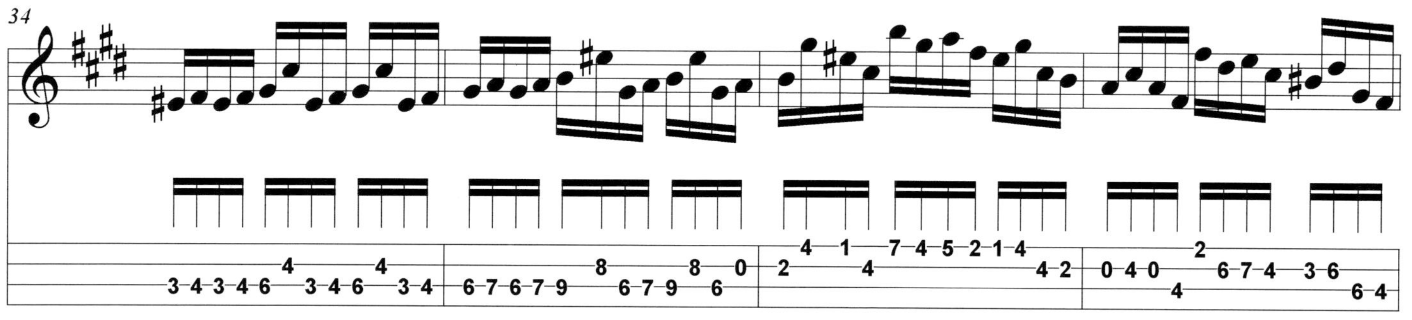

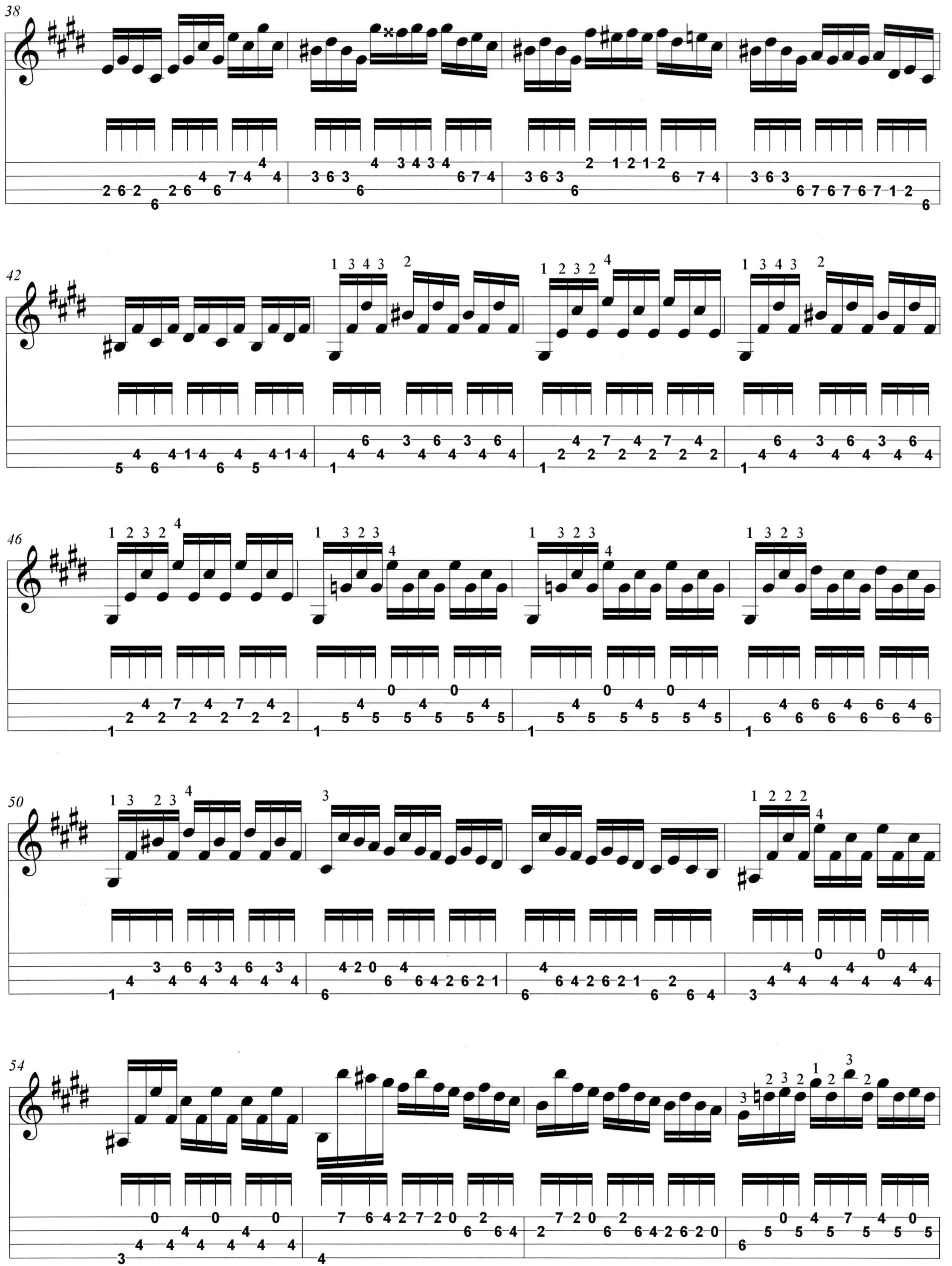

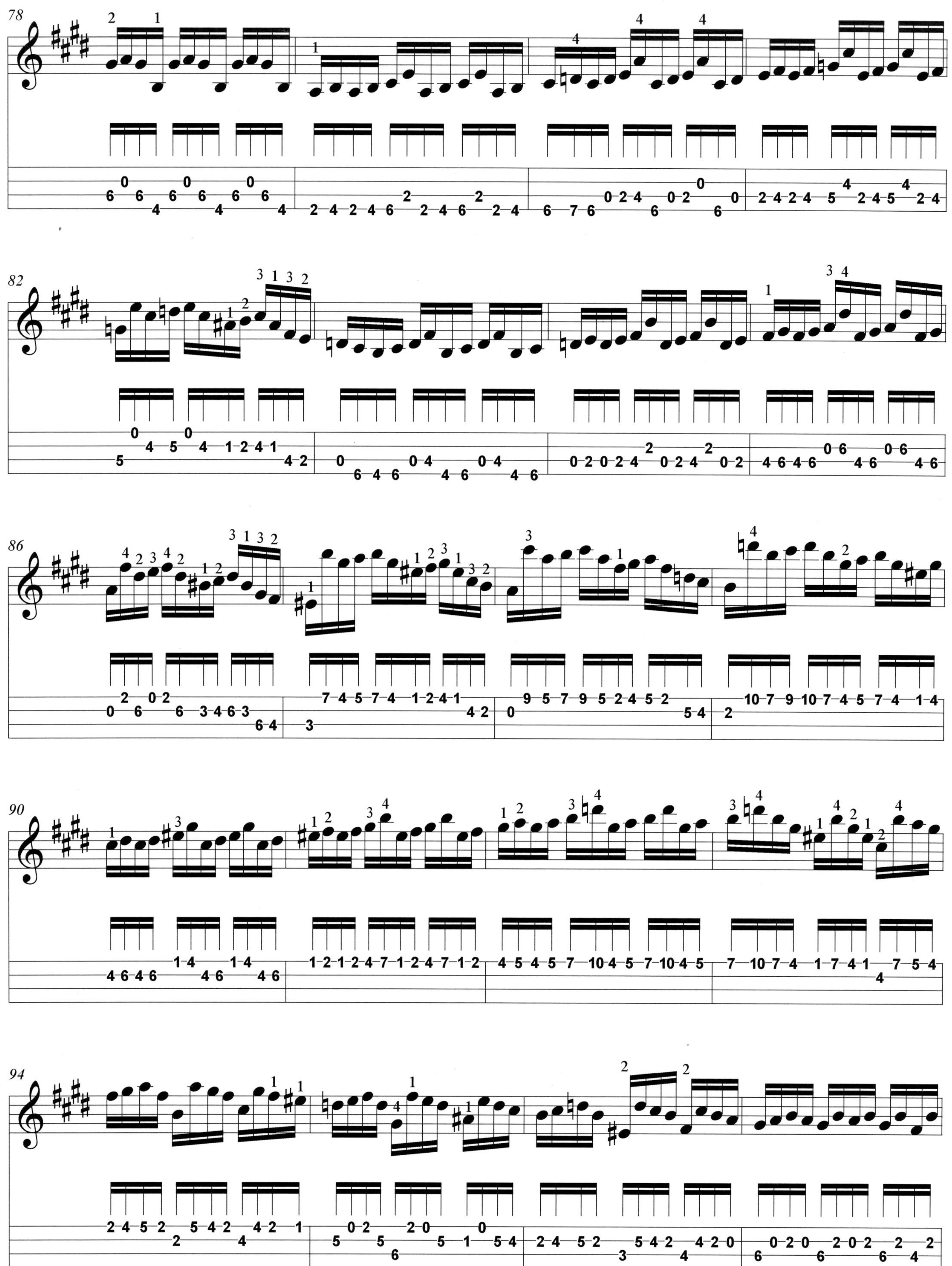

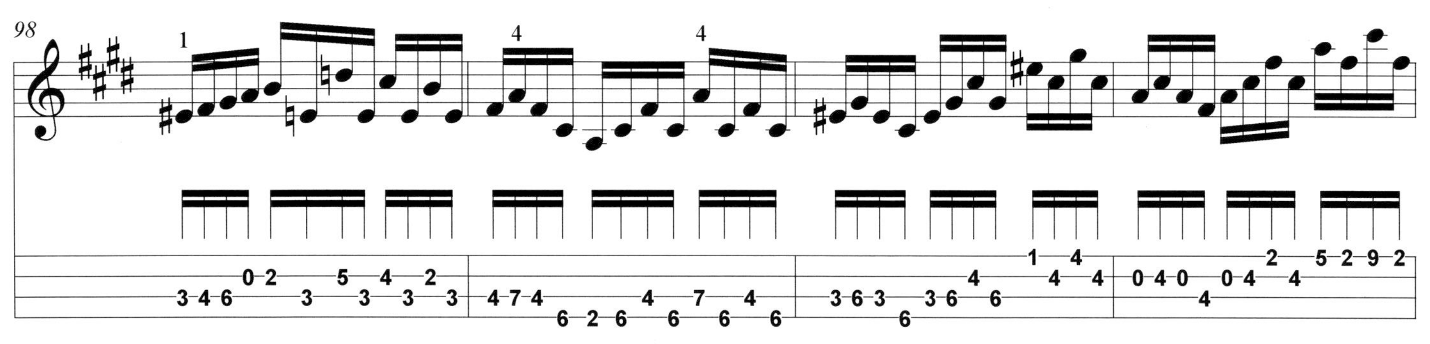

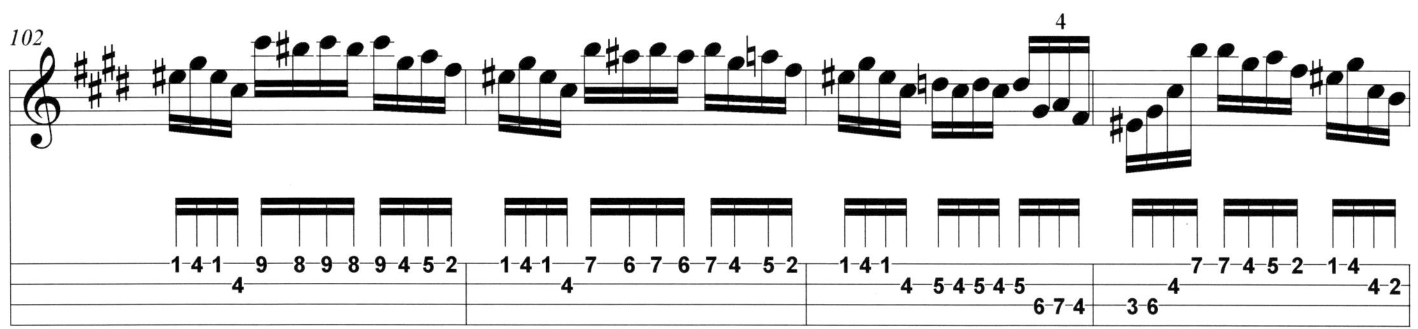

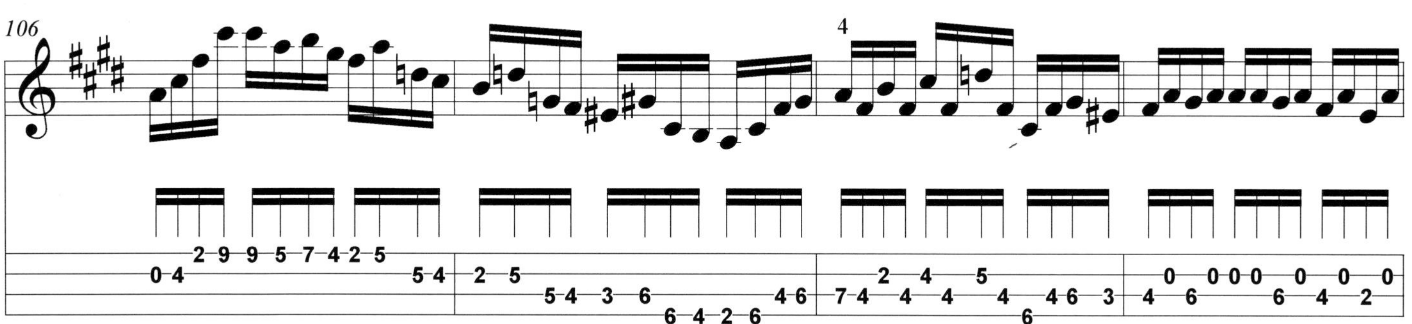

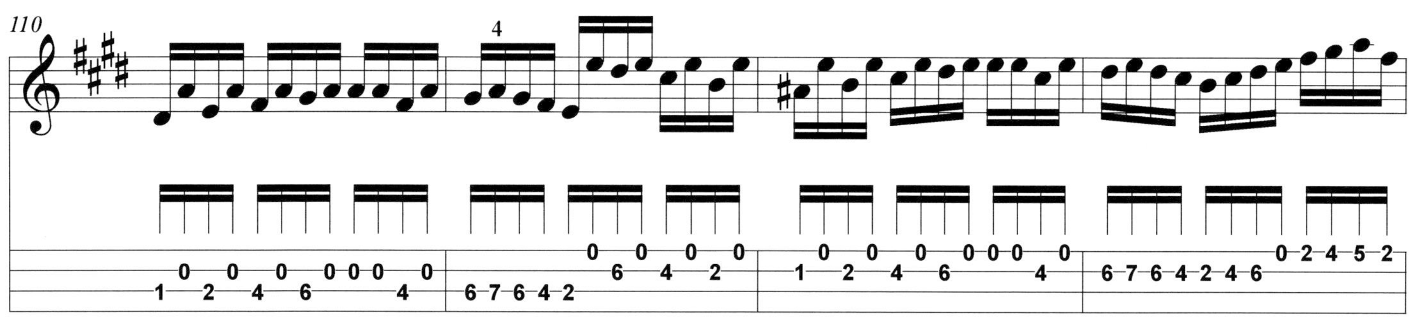

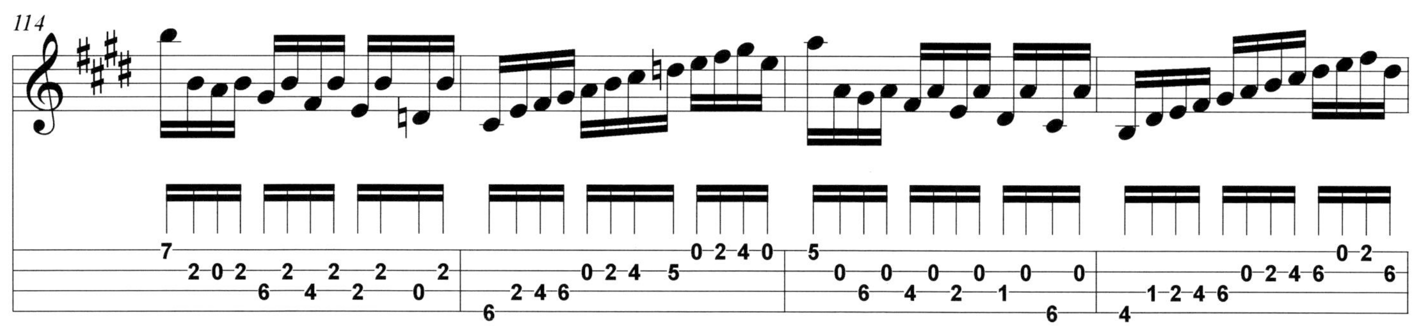

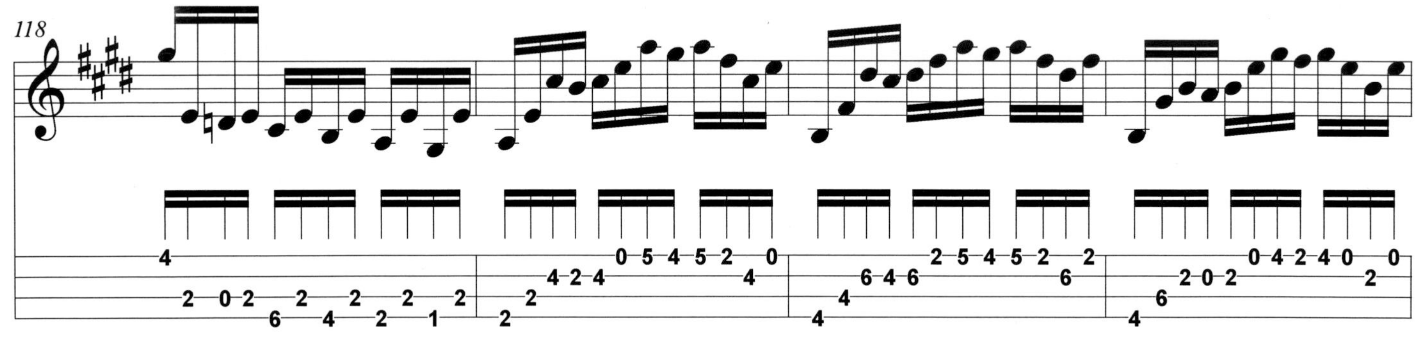
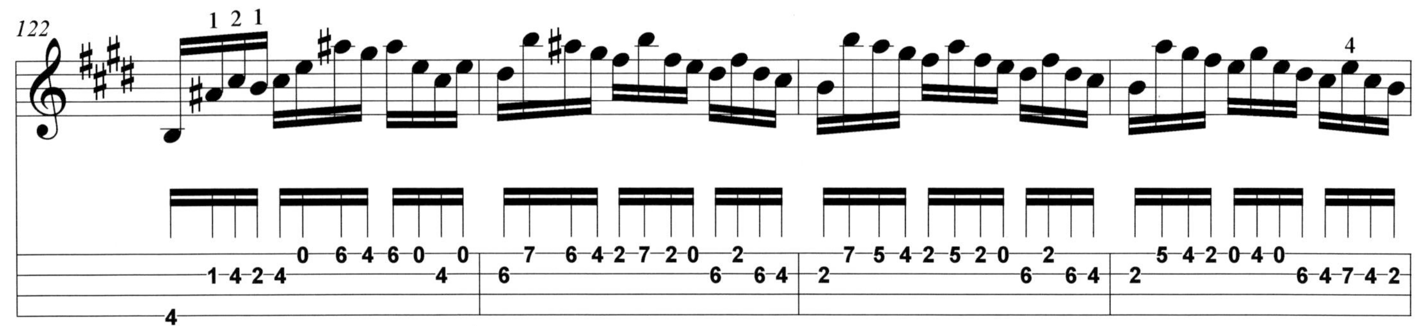
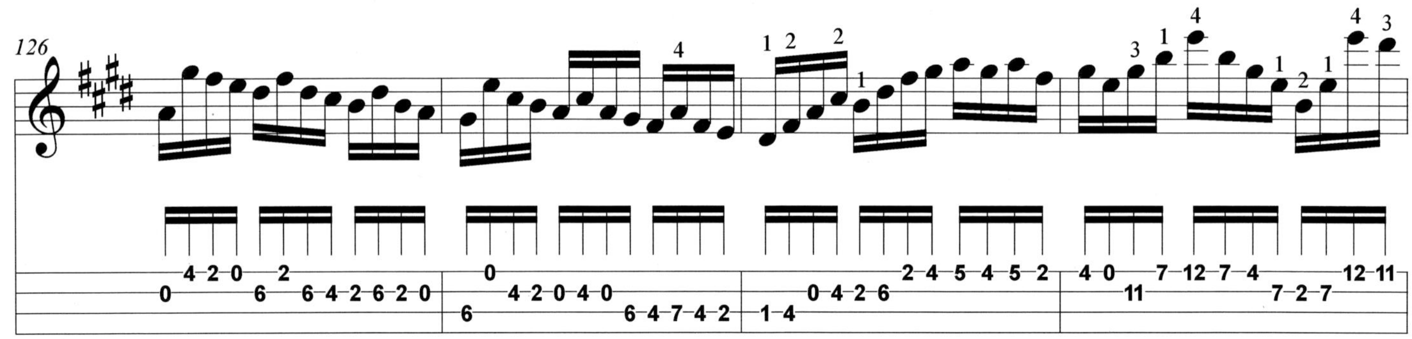
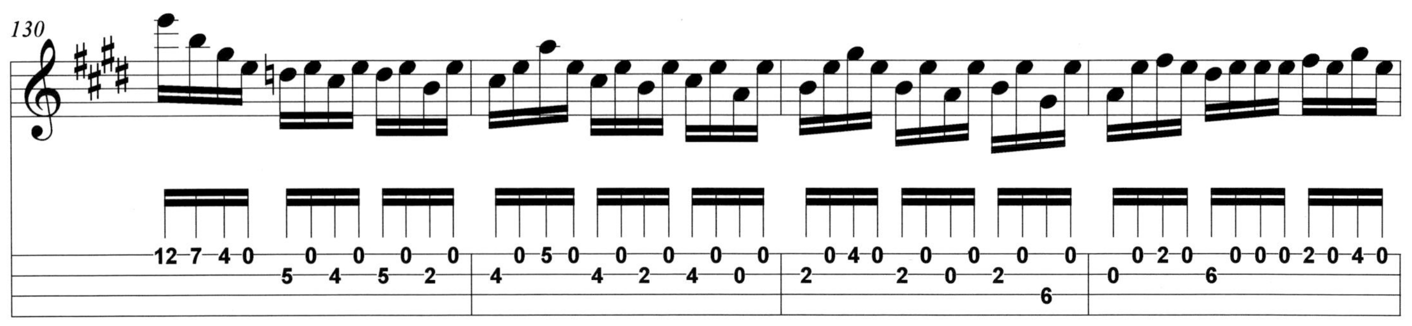
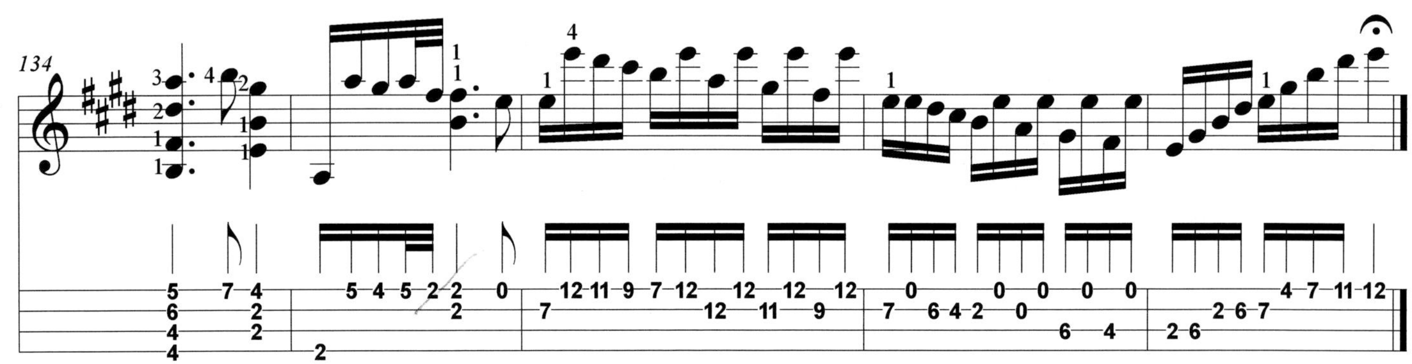